A Break-of-Day Book®

Ever since 1928, when Wanda Gág's classic *Millions of Cats* appeared, Coward, McCann & Geoghegan has been publishing books of high quality for young readers. Among them are the easy-to-read stories known as Break-of-Day books. This series appears under the colophon shown above—a rooster crowing in the sunrise—which is adapted from one of Wanda Gág's illustrations for *Tales from Grimm*.

Though the language used in Break-of-Day books is deliberately kept as clear and as simple as possible, the stories are not written in a controlled vocabulary. And while chosen to be within the grasp of readers in the primary grades, their content is far-ranging and varied enough to captivate children who have just begun crossing the momentous threshold into the world of books.

The Man Who
Loved Animals

Syd Hoff

Coward, McCann & Geoghegan, Inc.
New York

Library of Congress Cataloging in Publication Data
Hoff, Syd, 1912-
The man who loved animals.
Summary: A biography of the founder of the American
Society for the Prevention of Cruelty to Animals.
1. Animals, Treatment of—United States—Juvenile
literature. 2. Bergh, Henry, 181!-1888—Juvenile litera-
ture. 3. Social reformers—United States—Biography—
Juvenile literature. [1. Bergh, Henry, 1811-1888.
2. American Society for the Prevention of Cruelty to
Animals. 3. Animals—Treatment. 4. Reformers] I. Title.
HV4764.H63   179'.3'0924 [B] [92]   81-15168AACR2
ISBN 0-698-30737-2

In the 1860s, there were no laws
to protect animals and to punish
people who were cruel to them.
Tired horses were forced
to pull overcrowded streetcars,
and when they fell down,
no one took care of them.

Stray dogs were rounded up,
at fifty cents apiece,
and drowned. Nobody cared
if a cat lasted out the winter.

Sick cows were allowed to give milk.
When children drank the milk,
they got sick too.

Henry Bergh was rich and bored.
Then President Lincoln sent him
to be the head of the American office
in St. Petersburg, Russia.

"Maybe you will enjoy being a diplomat," said his wife, as they sailed for Europe.

Bergh bowed to other diplomats.
He gave them greetings
from the people of the United States.
He was glad to serve his country.
But he was still bored.

Then one day, in St. Petersburg,
Henry Bergh saw a peasant beating
his horse.
"Stop that at once!" he cried.

The peasant dropped his whip.
Bergh petted the horse.
For the first time in his life, he felt
that he had done something wonderful.
Whenever he saw a horse being beaten,
he ran to stop the beating.

"We must get laws passed
to protect animals.
In England, there's a Society for the
Prevention of Cruelty to Animals.
Maybe we can have one in America,"
he told his wife.

Bergh went back to New York
and visited all his friends.
"Will you please help me start
an American Society for the Prevention
of Cruelty to Animals?"
he asked.
"Sure, Henry, we'll help you,"
they said.

Henry Bergh made things happen.
In 1866 he got a permit to start
the American Society for the Prevention
of Cruelty to Animals, the ASPCA.
The first law making cruelty to animals
a crime was passed.
But Bergh found out that he had to do
all the work himself.
His wife was too ill to help him
and his friends were busy.

He started going around alone
looking for animals to help.

"Arrest that man!" he shouted,
when he saw someone beating a horse.

If a policeman didn't think
it was important enough,
Henry Bergh did the arresting himself.

18

He was only sorry when the judges
didn't give stiffer sentences.

Bergh,stopped streetcars
and made them carry lighter loads.

He designed a derrick to lift horses
that had fallen down,
and an ambulance to carry them away.

He even had drinking fountains
for horses installed on busy streets.

"They get thirsty too,"
he explained.

The ASPCA now had an office,
but it wasn't large enough.
Henry Bergh was always bringing in
stray cats and dogs.

"We'll keep them here until
we find new homes for them,"
he said.

He shouted at people
for wearing coats made of animal fur
and hats decorated with stuffed birds.

He stopped shows
that people went to
to see animals fight each other.
"Are you animals yourselves,
or human beings?" he asked.

One time a ship came into port
with a cargo of live turtles.
Bergh found the turtles
on their backs, unable to move.

Bergh arrested the captain and his entire crew.
"If I had my way, I'd arrange it
so none of you could move either,"
he said.

Another time, he stopped a wagon
on its way to market.
It was piled with sheep and pigs.
"Please don't let them suffer that way!"
cried Henry Bergh.
The driver and his helper laughed.

Bergh pulled both men off the wagon
and knocked their heads together.
"Now you know how those poor animals
must feel!" he said.

Newspapers made fun of Henry Bergh.
They called him "The Great Meddler."
That didn't stop him.
He went on looking for animals to protect.

He improved conditions in the zoo.
He got people to shoot at clay discs
instead of live pigeons.

He made sure farms and livestock
were inspected.
He made the milk and meat companies
work cleanly and without cruelty.
He had laws passed
protecting pigs and deer from hunters.
He stopped cruel experiments on animals.
He taught people, especially children,
to be kind.

But Henry Bergh also noticed
that children needed help.

"You can't stop me
from beating my own children,"
said a drunken father.
"I can and I will," said Bergh.

35

He had child beaters put in jail.
In 1875, after he helped to start
the Society for the Prevention
of Cruelty to Children,
Henry Bergh danced for joy.

"Children have the best hearts,
and make the best pet owners,"
he said, whenever they came
to adopt animals at an animal shelter.

One day Henry Bergh went to the circus.
He wanted to see how the animals were treated.

He didn't like the way they were trained.
He didn't like the way their cages were kept.

39

"You should treat your animals more kindly,"
he told P. T. Barnum, the circus owner.

Barnum had him thrown out of the circus.
The two men were bitter enemies for years.

Then, one night,
the straw in a tent caught fire.
Soon the whole circus was ablaze.

Animals died, though some escaped.
People were hurt too.

43

This happened several times.
Finally, P. T. Barnum said,
"Henry Bergh was right."
He gave his animals safer cages.
The two men became friends again.

The circus was better than ever.
Henry Bergh went to see it often.
He loved to sit with children
and enjoy the show.

Bergh spoke about kindness in many cities
all over the United States.
More and more people came to hear him.
The ASPCA grew and grew.

"Why do you worry so much about animals?"
someone asked at a meeting.

"If people learn to be kind to animals,
they will be kind to each other,"
Bergh replied.

Henry Bergh died in 1888,
during a great blizzard in New York.
Today, almost one hundred years later,
the ASPCA continues the job he started,
making the world a better place.